Introduction

During the summer of 2012 the eyes of the world were on Weymouth and Portland, Dorset, as it hosted the sailing events for the London 2012 Olympic and Paralympic Games.

Preparing for this momentous event took seven years of planning and hard work by Weymouth and Portland Borough, Dorset County and West Dorset District Councils, along with a wide range of partners and organisations.

The partners were determined to make the most of this once-in-a-lifetime opportunity, with key aims to:

- Provide the first ticketed spectator site for Olympic and Paralympic sailing;
- Ensure everyone had a safe and enjoyable experience;
- Raise the profile of the area, bringing long-term economic and tourism benefits.

Spectacular images of Weymouth Bay, Portland Harbour, the Jurassic Coast World Heritage Site, Weymouth's Georgian Esplanade, the Isle of Portland and the Nothe spectator site were beamed around the world, so the journey towards reaping those benefits has already begun.

This book aims to capture, in photographs, the atmosphere of the Games in Weymouth and Portland, Dorset, celebrating the part we all played in making the London 2012 Games such a tremendous success.

It was a huge privilege to host the Games, and we are grateful to all the Olympic authorities, the athletes and the thousands of visitors and local people for their enthusiasm and participation.

It truly was *A Summer to Remember*, and turning the pages of this wonderful book brings back the spirit and atmosphere of a year that many of us will never forget.

Councillor Angus Campbell
Chair Dorset 2012 Olympic Board

October 2012

100 DAYS TO GO

Weymouth's famous sand sculptor, Mark Anderson, created a huge sandcastle on Weymouth Beach to celebrate '100 days To Go' to the start of the Olympic Games.

THE TORCH COMES TO DORSET

The Torch relay arrived in Dorset on 12 July 2012, ending with the evening celebration on Weymouth Beach, on what seemed like the wettest day of the year!

After its arrival by boat from Portland, the honour of lighting the Olympic Cauldron was given to Di Ludlow, whose late husband Bill was the driving force behind the Weymouth and Portland National Sailing Academy.

Early next morning, the Torch left Portland Bill and travelled throughout the Borough cheered on by huge crowds, before making its way to the east of the County.

BATTLE OF THE WINDS

Battle of the Winds was the flagship event of the 'Maritime Mix' Cultural Olympiad celebrations; coordinated and presented by Cirque Bijou and Desperate Men.

They were accompanied by the 'Bridgwater Squibbers' and at the finale, the 2012 'Torch Waders' walked into the sea with lit torches, creating an amazing nightime spectacle.

TEAM GB
SAILING

On the day before the start of the Olympic sailing regatta, Team GB were saluted on Weymouth Beach Live Site and received a fantastic welcome from the thousands of people who came along to wish them all well in their sailing endeavours.

THE AMBASSADORS

Dressed in 'Pink & Purple', 530 Volunteer Ambassadors were the 'Welcoming Smile of Weymouth & Portland', meeting and greeting visitors to the Borough and guiding them on the 'Last Mile' to the Nothe ticketed site, the seafront and Live Site.

The Ambassadors were one of the great successes of the overall Games and their enthusiasm was appreciated by everyone.

SPORTS ARENAS

Over 100,000 people of all ages and abilities enjoyed sports taster session on the sports arenas on the beach during the Olympic and Paralympic Games, where a wide range of land and water based sports were offered including wheelchair basketball and sitting volleyball.

RACE DAYS

With 16 days of Olympic and 6 days of Paralympic sailing, the 2012 events in Weymouth & Portland were the largest taking place outside the London venues. The Nothe was the first official spectator site for Olympic Games sailing events, which not only provided a fantastic experience for ticket holders, but also meant that for the first time, the sailing athletes could see and hear the crowds cheering them on. Despite the poor weather in the lead up period, the area was blessed with sunny days and good sailing winds during both Games periods.

SUPER SUNDAY

An estimated 70,000 people came to cheer on Ben Ainslie in his successful attempt to secure his fourth consecutive Gold Medal, making Olympic Sailing history at his home Games. Excited crowds celebrated at both the Nothe ticketed site and the Beach Live Site.

MEDAL WINNERS

Ben Ainslie won his fourth successive Olympic Gold Medal and 4 Silver Medals were also won:

Gold - Finn
Silver - Star
Silver - 470 Women
Silver - 470 Men
Silver - RSX Men

Congratulations to all the Team GB athletes!

THE ORGANISATION

Over 500 staff from the three signatory authorities helped ensure that the local operations required to support the delivery of the sporting events were a success.

The Local Authority Operations Centre based at the Ferry Terminal close to Weymouth seafront, was the hub for coordinating crowd safety, the Ambassadors, the Live Site, Last Mile and other services.

TRANSPORT

A comprehensive Park & Ride service was provided for spectators and visitors by the Olympic Delivery Authority, bringing people in from Mount Pleasant and two car parks near Dorchester, Monkey Jump and Kingston Maurward. The purple double-decker shuttle buses became a familiar sight, ensuring that the roads into Weymouth remained clear and that difficulties over parking were kept to a minimum.

Shuttle bus

← Bays 3 4

FUN FOR ALL

As well as watching the Olympic sports on the large screens, thousands of people enjoyed the traditional entertainments on Weymouth's golden sands, including donkey rides and Punch & Judy, who were celebrating their 350th anniversary!

PARALYMPIC
GAMES

The Paralympic Flame was brought to Weymouth & Portland from London's Trafalgar Square by two local 'Flambassadors'. After arriving by boat from Portland, it was taken by land train along the seafront, and then put on show in the ICCI 360 Dome on Weymouth seafront, where it was viewed and photographed by many people.

Although there was no official spectator site for the Paralympic Games and the races were all held in Portland Harbour, locations such as Sandsfoot Gardens and Castle Cove became the informal viewing areas, creating a great international atmosphere. People with disabilities and friends and family of athletes were taken out by boat to see the sailing close up. The Team won the first Paralympic sailing medals ever for GB, with both Gold and Silver Medals secured.

THE MEDIA

At Games time a special Communications and Media Centre was set up in Weymouth Pavilion, which hosted over 350 national and international journalists. It provided information about the Games and the local area and provided easy access to the internet, allowing journalists to send their stories and images back to their home base.

THE VILLAGE

The athletes' village accommodated the Olympic & Paralympic athletes in properties that will become houses for sale and rent on Portland. Temporary buildings were brought in for catering, dining rooms and other essential operational facilities required by the London Organising Committee for the Olympic Games.

BUS TOP PARADE

On Carnival Day, just after the Olympic Games, an estimated 50,000 people lined the streets of Portland and Weymouth to cheer on Team GB and the medal winners. They travelled through the area and along Weymouth Seafront in an open top bus, followed by a huge crowd of Ambassador Volunteers – a real celebration and fantastic experience for both the athletes and jubilant public.

First published in 2012 by Weymouth & Portland Borough Council in association with The Dovecote Press, Stanbridge, Wimborne Minster, Dorset BH21 4JD.

ISBN 978-0-9573119-4-7

Photographers:
John Snelling (Studio Elite)
Geoff Moore (Dorset Media)
Barbara Jenkins
Karen Swan
Richard Langdon (Ocean Images)

Graphic Design:
Peter Van Allen

Media & Co-ordination:
Jacqui Gisborne
Lindsey Bell (RYA)

Editor:
Simon Williams

Printed in Spain by GraphyCems, Navarra

All papers used by The Dovecote Press are natural, recyclable products made from wood grown in sustainable, well-managed forests.